Early River Travel

Tim McNeese

Crestwood House
New York

Maxwell Macmillan Canada
Toronto

Maxwell Macmillan International
New York Oxford Singapore Sydney

Design: Deborah Fillion
Illustrations: © Chris Duke

Crestwood House
Macmillan Publishing Company
866 Third Avenue
New York, NY 10022

Maxwell Macmillan Canada, Inc.
1200 Eglinton Avenue East
Suite 200
Don Mills, Ontario, M3C 3N1

Macmillan Publishing Company is part of the
Maxwell Communication Group of Companies

First Edition

Printed in the United States of America

10 9 8 7 6 5 4 3 2 1

Library of Congress Cataloging-in-Publication Data

McNeese, Tim.
  Early River Travel : by Tim McNeese. — 1st ed.
      p.   cm.   — (Americans on the move.)
      Summary: Discusses the development and uses of different means of transportation along the great network of rivers in early America.
      ISBN 0-89686-733-1
      1. Inland water transportation—United States—History—Juvenile literature. 2. Riverboats—United States—History—Juvenile literature. [1. Inland water transportation—History. 2. Riverboats—History.] I. Title. II. Series: McNeese, Tim. Americans on the move.
      HE629.M36   1993
      386'.3'0973—dc20   91-42302

★

Contents

★

Early settlers relied upon the great American river system for shipping goods and transporting people.

★

Introduction

Travel in early America was very difficult and sometimes dangerous. Colonial roads were few and far between. They were poorly built and often muddy. Taking a wagon across those early trails was a hard trip indeed. As a result, many early colonists followed the example of the Indians and used America's vast river system to travel from place to place.

The greatest American river is the mighty Mississippi. Many other important rivers and **tributaries,** or river branches, come together with the Mississippi, creating a network of adjoining rivers. The Ohio, the Missouri and dozens of other rivers, along with the Mississippi, create a great river system. All together these rivers total an estimated 16,000 miles of navigable waters.

From the time of the earliest native American canoes to the invention of the steamboat, Americans used the large river system for shipping goods. They carried their families in crude boats to new lands. The story of these early forms of travel is an exciting tale of adventure and invention.

Each native American canoe was
designed to fit the needs of the tribe.

Earliest Forms of Rivercraft

Long before the first Europeans came to America, native Americans traveled on the great river and lake system. They used a type of watercraft called **canoe.** The different native American tribes, or nations, designed and built their own kinds of canoes. Two basic types of early canoes were the **dugout** and the **birchbark.**

Dugouts were made from a single log. Often a fallen tree was used, for such a log was usually well seasoned. Sometimes a live, standing tree was chosen. The American Indians would fell it by burning and chopping it with hatchets. Then they cut out a section of the tree trunk between 15 and 30 feet in length and 3 feet in diameter. Workers hollowed out the log section using cutting tools and fire. Because a canoe was carved out of a single piece of wood, it was very strong. It could be used on almost any river or lake. But it was very slow-moving in the water. These canoes were also too heavy to carry from river to river.

The birchbark canoe was more widely used by native Americans, especially the northern tribes. This canoe was made from bark peeled from standing trees. While birch was the favorite bark, spruce and elm were also used. Canoe builders obtained wide strips of bark by cutting a vertical line in the tree from the base to about their own height. Then they carefully peeled the bark sections from the tree. The canoe's framework was made from pieces of white cedar, because the wood splits easily. The birchbark covering was stretched around the framework and laced together with strips of split roots of black spruce. **Black spruce gum** was then heated until it became a thick syrup. This sap was applied to the canoe's seams and cracks, making the boat watertight. The canoe builder then lined the inside of the canoe with strips of white cedar. A set of bow-shaped strips of cedar was added to give the canoe a wider shape.

Each tribe had its own style of designing canoes. They were shaped differently and came in a variety of lengths. Generally, the birchbark canoes built in America ranged from 10 or 12 feet in length to as much as 50 or 60 feet. These canoes were fast, sleek and very mobile. An Indian warrior or hunter could travel hundreds of miles in such a boat. And, unlike the dugout variety, when a river became too shallow for the birchbark canoe, it could be easily picked up and carried. During a storm the Indian could turn the canoe over and use it for shelter. Early European explorers, missionaries, fur trappers and settlers used Indian-style canoes to travel on American rivers, although they sometimes changed the canoe design to suit their purposes.

The Need for New Types of Rivercraft

During the colonial period in America, most English colonists remained along the Atlantic coast. For many decades only the bravest and most adventurous dared to travel across the Appalachian Mountains into the **Ohio Valley.** In fact, the British government passed a law called the **Proclamation of 1763,** which made it illegal for English colonists to travel across the mountains. This act stated that all the land that was between the Appalachians and the Mississippi River was for the Indians. Some explorers, such as Daniel Boone, ignored the law and went west to open up such wilderness areas as Kentucky and Tennessee.

But by the 1780s, after the Revolutionary War, the United States was born. And the new Americans did not have to worry about the old Proclamation of 1763. When the United States passed the **Northwest Ordinance** in 1787, the lands of what were to become the western states of Ohio, Indiana, Illinois, Michigan and Wisconsin were open for pioneers. Suddenly, America was a much bigger place. Almost immediately its new people saw the need for better kinds of transportation.

Over the next 30 or 40 years, hundreds of thousands of Americans moved into the national interior. They occupied land all the way to the Mississippi River and beyond. Many of these early emigrants traveled on the same rivers, streams and lakes that the native Americans had paddled along for hundreds of years.

As these western pioneers were mostly farmers, they grew crops and raised hogs and cattle that needed to be sold. For many of these farmers, the cheapest way to get such goods to market was to float them down the western river system to the great port at New Orleans.

★

This period of American history, from the 1780s through the great Mississippi steamboat years before the Civil War, saw many different kinds of rivercraft used on the western rivers. Perhaps the most important types were flatboats and keelboats. These two types of rivercraft carried much of the farm produce raised by Ohio Valley farmers.

Flatboats

The first flatboats could be found on the Ohio River. Such a boat was built for rivers because its flat bottom allowed it to float safely in as little as a few feet of water. A flatboat was not really a boat. It was a big, floating box, which almost anyone with the right tools would build. It had a rectangular shape. Its sides stood about 5 feet high. Flatboats came in different sizes, according to their purposes. They ranged in length from 20 to 100 feet and were 10 to 25 feet wide. The aver-

Flatboats were commonly used for shipping goods and produce along American rivers.

age flatboat was 12 to 14 feet wide and nearly 50 feet long. Ohio flatboats needed to be this size to allow them to pass through the falls of the Ohio River, near Louisville, Kentucky. In the 19th century these falls, or rapids, were just about 15 feet wide. Any larger rivercraft had a difficult time passing through these chutes.

Flatboats were meant to float a farmer's produce downstream only. They were almost never used to carry anything or anyone back up a river. Most flatboats were controlled by three long **sweeps,** or large paddles. They were also called **broadhorns.** One sweep was located at the rear, or **stern,** of the boat. A fourth and smaller sweep, or oar, was sometimes placed at the bow, or front of the flatboat. Named the **gouger,** this sweep was just another aid in helping steer the boat downriver. The other two sweeps were placed on

★

either side. Such a flatboat, when fully loaded, usually sat about two feet deep in the water.

All flatboats had a deck area where produce was stored and the crew lived during the long trip to New Orleans. A larger flatboat had a small cabin located in its center. Here the crew could sleep and sometimes cook. Because of their rough-hewn lumber construction, the sides of most flatboats could stop a bullet fired from shore. This was important to flatboaters, who worried about Indian or river-pirate attack. Often, a flatboat's sides featured loopholes that allowed flatboaters to fire on attackers while protected.

The average flatboat could carry lots of western farm produce. As many as 400 to 500 barrels or crates could be crowded on the boat's deck. Items shipped on western flatboats included fruits, vegetables and livestock, such as cattle, chickens and hogs. Even slaves were shipped downriver to be sold at the markets in Natchez, Mississippi, or New Orleans. When these flatboats reached their downriver destination, they were sold for the lumber. Many of New Orleans's early sidewalks were built from flatboat lumber.

Life on a flatboat went at a slow pace. The average flatboat needed a five-person crew to work the sweeps and do the cooking. The cooking was often done on deck on a fire built over a sandbox. Floating down the Ohio and Mississippi rivers from Pittsburgh to New Orleans was nearly a 2,000 mile trip. The voyage took between five and six weeks, with the boat traveling 24 hours a day. A trip from Louisville, Kentucky, to New Orleans required a month on the rivers.

During the early decades of the 1800s, between 400 and 700 flatboats arrived in New Orleans each year. The year 1847 was the busiest for flatboats. That year, more than 2,600 flatboats took the trip from the

Ohio River to New Orleans. Certainly, hundreds more landed at ports farther upriver. From that date on, the number of flatboats traveling to New Orleans dropped. Many western farmers had their goods shipped downriver on steamboats instead.

When the farmers finished their float to New Orleans and sold their goods, they then began the long trip home. Most took passage on a steamboat up the

Natchez Trace was an important trade and travel route for flatboat crew members during the early 1800s.

★

Mississippi River to Natchez, Mississippi. From there they took the famous Natchez Trace, an overland road which ran from Natchez to Nashville, Tennessee. This was the only well-traveled road across the old southwestern state of Mississippi. Between the years 1800 and 1820, the Natchez Trace saw the most human traffic. This 450-mile walk was difficult. Travelers often became sick in the swamps or were attacked by Indians and robbers. Walking back up the trace might take six to eight weeks.

Keelboats

Another western rivercraft was the keelboat. This boat was very different from a flatboat, since it was a permanent craft. It was much more expensive to build than a flatboat, costing between $2,000 and $3,000. Keelboats had "professional" crews which carried western goods downriver for a fee. Typically, a keelboat could deliver a ton of cargo upriver cheaper than it could be carried overland by wagon.

A keelboat was built with a 4-inch square strip of timber running from bow to stern called a keel. The boats were generally 60 to 70 feet long and featured a cargo hold 3 or 4 feet deep. The boats were pointed at both the bow and the stern. A box-shaped cabin covered the center of the deck. Keelboats usually had a center mast with a sail. Most keelboats needed a crew of about ten.

On each side of the keelboat's deck was a walkway where the crew could "pole" the boat upriver. To do this, each person would take a turn pushing a long pole into the river bottom and "walking" the boat upstream. These setting poles were usually about 12 to 14 feet long and capped with iron. This was very difficult work.

★

Cleats were nailed across the walkway to give the polers something to push against as they walked. If the river current was too strong, the crew was forced to **cordelle** the boat. By this method, the crew used long ropes tied to a tree onshore and pulled the boat upstream.

The keelboat was one of the most popular types of early American rivercraft.

★

Working as a professional keelboater was a hard job. Such workers were often rough and tough. Perhaps the most legendary keelboater was Mike Fink. Born in 1780, near Pittsburgh, Fink served as a scout in the American Indian wars. Later, he owned and operated two keelboats. Fink was a great bragger. He would challenge anyone to a variety of contests. His famous boasts often went like this: "I'm a salt river roarer! I'm a ringtailed squealer! I'm half wild horse and half cock-eyed alligator and the rest o' me is crooked snags an' every lick I make in the woods lets in an acre o' sunshine. I can outrun, outjump, outshoot, outbrag, outdrink an' outfight, rough-an'-tumble, no holds barred, any man on both sides of the river from Pittsburgh to New Orleans an' back again to St. Louee. Come on, you flatters, you bergers, you milk-white mechanics an' see how tough I am to chaw! I ain't had a fight for two days an' I'm spilin' for exercise! Cock-a-doodle-doo!" Fink's river career lasted from 1790 to 1822. That year he was shot by a companion during a fur-trading expedition on the Missouri River.

Other Important Rivercrafts

While flatboats and keelboats were the two most popular kinds of early American rivercrafts, there were other boats on the rivers. Many of these were built for very special jobs. Some were simply variations on flatboats and keelboats. Some had names associated with the specific rivers they were used on.

Some of the more important boats included pirogues, batteaus, mackinaws, Durham boats and arks. A *pirogue* is a very large canoe, approximately 50 feet long and about 8 feet wide. This boat could carry a pioneer family and all its household goods. A *skiff* is a wide boat with a flat bottom constructed out of planks. Skiffs were usually tied to bigger boats, such as flatboats and keelboats, and used to row the crew ashore. A *batteau*, also spelled *bateaux*, was a very large skiff. It could also carry a family and goods. It was steered downstream by several pairs of sweeps. These boats were also poled back upstream.

Far western rivercraft used by fur trappers were called *mackinaw*. They were often 60 feet long and 15 feet wide. The mackinaw had rounded or pointed sides. The boat was built on a platform of logs and featured vertical sides. It was used to carry a large cargo of animal hides downriver for sale.

A *Durham* boat was a keelboat shaped like a birchbark canoe. It was named after Robert Durham of Pennsylvania, who built river vessels back east around 1750. This boat was used heavily on the Delaware River.

Arks were used on the Susquehanna and Delaware rivers in Pennsylvania. These boats became popular on the Ohio and Mississippi rivers after the Northwest Territory Indian wars. They were usually from 75 to 100 feet long and 15 to 20 feet wide. The ark was built out of heavy timbers and lumber planks and cost about $100. The bow and stern were pointed in a V-shape. Arks only floated downstream, and steering was provided by a 40-foot-long sweep.

Mohawk or *Schenectady* boats were keelboats built and used on the Mohawk or Schenectady rivers. *Kentucky* or *New Orleans* boats were flatboats used on rivers in these two areas.

The *Ohio packet boat* was a large keelboat, with a passenger cabin, measuring from 75 to 100 feet long by 15 to 20 feet wide. It featured a mast and sails and used many polers. These packets were able to carry

★

passengers and freight and ran between Pittsburgh and Louisville.

All the different kinds of rivercraft listed above were important for carrying western goods, passengers, or both. Some of them were limited to just floating downstream. Others needed the wind to push the boat's sail or had to be pulled upstream by strong crews. This kind of work was very difficult. And travel on all these boats was generally very slow.

But during this same period of time, from the 1780s to the 1860s, some inventors were working very hard to develop a completely new kind of boat. This boat was to be powered by a steam engine and paddle wheels. These **steamboats,** as they were called, changed the way Americans traveled on their western rivers and lakes.

Probably the most famous American connected with the invention of the steamboat is Robert Fulton. He is remembered for his steamboat, the *Clermont.* But Fulton did not invent the steamboat. Several other inventors in both America and Europe worked on building a boat powered by a steam engine before and during the time of Fulton.

Perhaps the most important name among these early steamboat builders was a hardworking fellow named John Fitch. He did more to bring about a successful steamboat in America than any other inventor. In fact, Fitch designed and built the first working steamboat to offer passenger service in America. But Fitch saw many disappointments during his years as a steamboat designer. His story is a sad one with many failures, even after he had proved to the nation that a steamboat could be a practical way to travel.

The mackinaw was a flat-bottomed boat
with a pointed bow and a square stern.

★

John Fitch Builds
a Steamboat

Fitch was born in 1743 on a small farm outside Windsor, Connecticut. As a teenager he was apprenticed to a watchmaker, who promised to teach him the trade. The watchmaker wasted the boy's time and did not really help young Fitch learn the art of watchmaking. This disappointment was one of many Fitch was to face over the years.

He spent the next several years teaching himself how to repair clocks, working during the American Revolution fitting bayonets on patriot muskets and selling trade goods to American soldiers. Near the end of the war, he traveled all over the newly expanded United States. In 1780 he walked across Pennsylvania and took a boat down the Ohio River to Kentucky. While in Kentucky, Fitch was captured by Indians. He was held captive for two years until he managed to escape. He did some surveying and walked as far as the Great Lakes.

These years of travel gave Fitch a clear picture of the many rivers and lakes found across the young

United States, which stretched west to the Mississippi. Many ideas swirled in Fitch's head, but the dream of inventing a steamboat kept coming back to him again and again.

When Fitch actually began to plan his steamboat, it looked very different from anything else on the water at that time. In fact, it would look nothing like the great Mississippi riverboats that were decades away from being built. His idea centered on two sprocket wheels connecting a chain loop. These wheels were attached to a set of vertical paddles which were to stroke across the water, pushing the boat forward.

Building a Working Model

Fitch began his work by building a model of his plan. He tried out the 2-foot-long model in a small stream, and it worked! But building a full-scale boat required money. He needed a large steam engine to power his boat. Fitch took his idea to some important people, including George Washington and Benjamin Franklin, to gain their support for his steamboat. He even presented his dream to the new American Congress. But he had no luck.

Finally, the state of New Jersey agreed to allow Fitch to operate any steamboat he might build on any New Jersey rivers. This permission meant that any future steamboats in New Jersey were to be built only by Fitch and no one else. Once Fitch received this state grant, some Philadelphia investors agreed to give him $300 to build a one-person experimental boat. This boat would not have a steam engine, but Fitch was to demonstrate how his paddle and endless-chain idea might work.

By the spring of 1786, Fitch, with the help of a

★

21

mechanic named Henry Voight, launched his boat on the Delaware River. Fitch was seated in the boat, ready to turn the cranks that were to make his strange-looking craft push through the water. But something went wrong. The boat zigzagged all over the river. The cranks did not work properly. The boat jerked Fitch every way, making him and his boat look foolish. The experiment was a failure.

But Fitch was not finished with his dreams for a steamboat. He abandoned the chain-and-sprocket idea. Instead, he decided to build a boat with two sets of oars on each side. These oars were to be attached vertically to a metal framework. Through a series of cranks, these oar sets could take turns paddling. Fitch and Voight went straight to work. They first built a working model. Then they built a one-person skiff. They built a miniature steam engine, which they added to the small boat.

Just a few months after their first disaster on the Delaware, Fitch and Voight put their second boat into the water. Their boat looked very strange to the people who watched on that July day. But Fitch and Voight were happy. Their new design worked!

However, John Fitch needed more money. He had still not built a full-scale working steamboat. To help him find backers for such a boat, Fitch went to the state legislatures of Delaware, Pennsylvania, New York and Virginia. These states granted him the sole privilege of operating steamboats on their rivers, just as New Jersey had a few years earlier. With such exclusive grants, Fitch was able to raise enough money through investors to build his boat.

John Fitch dreamed of building a boat that
would change the way Americans traveled.

★

Fitch's designs seemed strange in comparison with other boats of the time.

Another Failure

Fitch's plans called for building a boat 40 feet long, with an 11-foot beam. The boat was expected to sit nearly 4 feet in the water. The boat's engine needed a piston 12 inches in diameter. By June of 1787, Fitch's large steamboat was ready for a test.

But the test run, which took place in Philadelphia, was another disappointment for Fitch. The boat went a slow 2 1/2 miles an hour upstream. The rudder did not work right, and, at a turn in the river, Fitch ran his boat aground on a mudbank. Once again, Fitch and Voight were the objects of everyone's laughter.

Fitch, however, did not let his dream die. He spent the next year reworking his boat. But money was tight for Fitch. He spent nearly everything he had on redesigning his steamboat. He barely ate and his clothes went to rags. But by the summer of 1788, his and Voight's boat was ready for another public launch.

This time, everything began perfectly. The paddles worked and the steamboat skimmed quickly over the water. Mile after mile slipped past as Fitch's new steamboat sped on toward its destination, 20 miles upriver to Burlington. Soon, Fitch could see his goal in the distance as Voight fed more and more wood into the steam engine's firebox. The boat had hit top speed, and the steam engine stroked its piston faster and faster. On the Burlington dock, hundreds of people waited to greet Fitch's boat.

Then, with typical Fitch luck, something went wrong. Voight had worked up such a head of steam in the boat's engine that the pressure had cracked its seams. The two steamboat builders knew nothing about pressure safety valves. As a result of the accident, the engine quit, and the boat slowed to a stop. It

★

began floating back down the river, pushed by the current. And the boat had been only a few hundred yards from reaching the Burlington dock.

Success at Last!

For two more years, Fitch and his friend Voight worked to improve their steamboat. Then, in early summer 1790, their boat was successfully launched. This boat was 45 feet long. An iron boiler and firebox sat in the boat's midsection. A cylinder 12 inches in diameter powered 12 paddles, 6 on each side. A tall smokestack carried the smoke away from the passengers. Forward of the smokestack was a small passenger cabin. The boat clipped along at a rate of 8 miles an hour. That summer Fitch's boat made 31 trips on the Delaware River, three times a week, carrying passengers from Arch Street in Philadelphia to Trenton, New Jersey. The trip was 40 miles long. The cost of the trip: five shillings—about $1.25. Before the end of the summer, Fitch had taken his boat a total of more than 1,000 miles. There were no serious engine problems. The man who had spent four years in the face of public ridicule was pleased with his boat's performance. But still, Fitch's boat was destined for failure.

Although his boat worked, Fitch did not receive continued support from his financial backers. Nor did he have the support of the public. Fitch's problem was no longer finding a way to build a working steamboat. Instead, he had to face the problem of having created something people were not ready to accept. Fitch and his steamboat were ahead of their time. Soon Fitch's financial support dried up, the regular passenger service dwindled and his dream sank into the waters of the Delaware River.

★

A Sad End

Fitch spent his final years working in Boston and New York on the docks. He quietly continued his work on steamboats. He designed a small boat that was propelled by a rotating screw. The idea was far ahead of its time. Such a screw propeller was used on great ocean liners a century later. But Fitch's ideas went unnoticed. In time, Fitch left the East and traveled to the Ohio country. He took up residence in Bardstown, Kentucky. In his boardinghouse room, he built a model steamboat. But no one was interested in Fitch's new dream—steam traffic on the Ohio River. Sick and depressed, Fitch decided to end his sad life. On a summer night in 1798, he took an overdose of medication.

He was buried behind the Bardstown jail, on the banks of the Ohio River, in an unmarked grave. Ironically, a generation later, the Ohio became one of the busiest rivers in America for a new type of river travel—steamboating.

The Clermont, the steamboat built by Robert Fulton

Robert Fulton, Master Inventor

The story of Robert Fulton and his steamboat, the *Clermont,* is an exciting one. Remember: Fulton did not invent the steamboat. Many others in both America and Europe worked on such boats. As explained in the previous chapter, John Fitch designed and built a steam-powered boat that carried passengers in 1790. Fulton made an important contribution, however. He was the first American to design and build a steamboat that earned a profit carrying passengers and cargo. But Fulton's days of inventing did not begin with his steamboat.

Robert Fulton was born in Lancaster County, Pennsylvania, in 1765. Already, crews were working on boats powered by steam. But as a young man, Robert did not show any interest in anything called a steamboat. In fact, young Fulton had a strong interest in becoming an artist and painter.

At age 21, Fulton went to England to study art.

★

From Painting to Inventing

While working under the great American painter Benjamin West, Fulton began to show an interest in mechanical things. Steam engines were being built, and textile factories were operated by these machines. Soon, Fulton began his career as an inventor of many different kinds of machines. After 1793 he gave up his art career. From that year on, Fulton painted only as a hobby. Through his interest in mechanics, young Robert designed and built a hemp-twisting machine for making rope and a marble-cutting device.

But for the next 15 years, Fulton concentrated his efforts on inventing new kinds of boats. His interest in steamboats came later, however. First, Fulton worked on making improvements in canal systems. During the 1780s and 1790s, many new canals were being built in England and in America. Canal fever was sweeping through both nations. Robert Fulton's inventions included new ways of building canals and new kinds of canal boats. He designed new types of lock systems

★

American pioneers traveled along the rivers in steamboats, searching for new areas to call home.

used in canals. Among his canal boat designs were a market boat, a dispatch boat (for express service on canals) and a trader boat. Developing these new canal boats helped Fulton later when he began work on steamboats.

Then came Fulton's interest in a new kind of watercraft—the submarine. For nearly ten years—from 1797 to 1806—Fulton focused on designing, building and testing an underwater submersible. He built a working submarine device and invented torpedoes capable of blowing up sailing ships. Fulton's submarine could dive, surface and fire torpedoes. Fulton had trouble, however, perfecting a way of propelling his submarine. In 1801 Fulton demonstrated his new weapon for the French ruler Napoleon. When the French showed a limited interest, Fulton crossed the English Channel and demonstrated his submarine for the British admiralty. But soon his interest in submarines was to take a back seat to another inventive challenge—building a steamboat.

★

Robert Livingston

To explain how Fulton became involved in designing steamboats, we must now turn to the work of another famous American, Robert Livingston. He was an important political leader. During the Revolutionary War, he was a member of the Continental Congress. Livingston served on the committee which drafted the final wording of the Declaration of Independence. From 1777 to 1801, he was the chancellor of New York State. In 1798 Livingston administered the oath of office to America's first president, George Washington.

During the 1790s, Livingston became interested in steamboats. In 1794 a Connecticut man named Samuel Morey built and ran a steamboat from Hartford, Connecticut, to New York City. Livingston was excited by Morey's boat and rode the craft. He realized that there was a definite future for steam-powered boats in America, and he wanted to be a part of it. Livingston did some steamboat research of his own. He even convinced the state of New York to take away John Fitch's monopoly on running steamboats on New York's rivers and give it to him.

In 1801 Livingston left America and his steamboat research. He had been named United States minister to France. And it was the next year, 1802, that the paths of Robert Livingston and Robert Fulton came together.

Partners

Fulton had begun his studies and experiments on steamboats before meeting Livingston. As early as 1793, Fulton built a steamboat model which was pushed along by a spring shaped like a fish tail. But the model moved with great jerks, and Fulton abandoned the idea. By the next year, he created an original design for steamboat **propulsion.** He dreamed of side paddles that rotated as they scooped the water, pushing the boat along. He tested his idea on many different models. Finally, by November 1794, Fulton ordered a steam engine. He continued his experiments but did not have the money to build an actual full-scale steamboat.

When Fulton met Robert Livingston in 1802, he gained the opportunity to build the boat he dreamed of. He and Livingston formed a partnership. Livingston agreed to raise the money Fulton needed. He provided Fulton with $2,500. This was enough to build a boat.

Fulton began work on his first steamboat in 1803. It was 70 feet long and 8 feet wide. He and Livingston agreed to rent a steam engine rather than wait months for one to be built in England. Fulton and a crew of mechanics worked on the banks of the Seine River in Paris. They spent long days constructing the boat and preparing it for a steam engine.

Robert Fulton

Robert Livingston

But things did not go well for Robert Fulton. The day before he planned to take his new steamboat out for a test run, tragedy struck. The steam engine was too heavy for the boat. Fulton's craft had broken in two and sunk to the bottom of the river. He and his crew spent the rest of the night trying to rescue the expensive steam engine from the dark water.

A Successful Test

Fulton did not quit, however. His boat was rebuilt, and on August 9, 1803, Fulton tested his steamboat on the

★

Seine. The dock was crowded with people watching the new steamboat. Among them were officials of the French navy. They were very interested in the new design. They knew about Robert Fulton, the submarine builder. And they wanted to see if his latest invention should be taken seriously.

At about six o'clock that evening, the steam engine was fired up. The boat began moving upriver under its own power. The great side wheels turned and paddled the water. For the next hour and a half, Robert Fulton showed the people of Paris how a steamboat could work. He demonstrated how his boat could run, stop, turn, even tow other boats. The steamboat achieved, however, a disappointing speed of only 3 miles an hour. Fulton had hoped for at least 10 miles an hour. But he had managed to impress those French navy officials watching from the docks along the Seine. When they reported back to Napoleon about what they had seen that evening, he is said to have cried, "This is capable of changing the face of the world!"

Trouble with England

Not long after his steamboat's successful Paris trial run, Fulton received an offer from the British government. But it was not about a steamboat. The British were interested in Fulton's submarine! The government wanted Fulton to sell the plans for his underwater war machine. Fulton agreed to build the British a submarine and sell the invention to them for an amount equal to $500,000.

But despite their interest, British government officials made things difficult for Fulton. They made him wait for their decision. At the same time, Fulton was making plans to return to America. As part of his agreement with Robert Livingston, Fulton had promised to build two steamboats. Their contract required Fulton to build a second boat in America on the Hudson River in New York, once he had built a successful boat in France. After his steamboat's successful run in Paris, Fulton had turned his eyes to America and to plans for his second boat.

He ordered a second steam engine from Boulton and Watt, a company that made the best steam engines in England. But the British government refused to allow Fulton to ship his steam engine to America. They wanted to keep him in England, building a submarine. Fulton was, therefore, at the mercy of English officials. They wanted to pay Fulton less than he wanted for his submarine plans, and they were willing to hold up his American steamboat plans to do so.

For many months, the British government kept Fulton involved in building torpedoes. Fulton came to realize that the British were not really interested in having a submarine built. They just wanted to keep him from building one for the French.

Finally, a break came for Fulton. On October 21, 1805, the English navy defeated the French at the Battle of Trafalgar. This victory made England the most powerful naval force in the world. Soon the government cared little about Robert Fulton and his submarine. They allowed him to leave England and go to America. The government even let Boulton and Watt deliver to the United States the steam engine Fulton so desperately needed. By the fall of 1806, Robert Fulton was on his way back to America. It had been 20 years since he left his native country.

★

Fulton was anxious to return home and introduce Americans to a new and exciting way to travel.

★

The *Clermont*

After landing in America, Robert Fulton went straight to work building his second steamboat. He intended to make this boat better than the one he had built in Paris. After the successful test run in 1803, Fulton had studied the work of other steamboat builders and dreamers. Fulton had even seen John Fitch's steamboat plans. Fitch had brought his plans to Paris in 1790. Fulton saw the plans through a third party, and he studied them in detail. He and Fitch probably never actually met.

Fulton set up shop in the shipyard of Charles Browne on the East River in New York City. The disassembled Boulton and Watt steam engine was delivered in separate crates. Fulton put the engine back together.

His new boat was to be 150 feet long and 13 feet wide. It was to draw about 2 feet of water. Obviously, it would be much larger than the boat he had built three years earlier in Paris. It was to have two paddle wheels built slightly ahead of the boat's center. A low cabin was added to the boat and a railing built around the deck. Fulton had seats built on the boat's deck for passengers. Many jealous sailors and dockhands watched Fulton and his mechanics building the strange-looking boat and made fun of it. They called it "Fulton's Folly." Actually, they must have known that Fulton was on to something, because these same sailors tried to sabotage his boat. They tore up equipment and destroyed parts of the boat during nighttime raids. Fulton even had to hire a night watchman.

While the boat was under construction, Fulton's partner, Robert Livingston, often visited the docks to watch the boat's progress. Fulton, in fact, was to name the steamboat after Livingston's country estate on the Hudson River—Clermont-on-the-Hudson. (Fulton had originally named his boat the *North River Steamboat*.)

Finally, work on the *Clermont* was completed. On August 9, 1807, Fulton secretly took his new steamboat out on the East River for a test run. It was four years to the day that he had tested his first boat on the Seine in Paris. Fulton steamed his boat up the East River for a mile. He experimented with different numbers of blades on the boat's paddle wheels, looking for the number which gave his craft the best speed. Happy with the day's trials, he returned to make plans for the *Clermont's* first voyage.

Sailing Up the Hudson

Thousands of curious people lined the docks of New York Harbor on the day Fulton planned to take the *Clermont* up the Hudson River. It was a Monday, August 17, 1807. The voyage was to begin in the North River, near the state's prison. Fulton intended to steam up the Hudson River all the way to the state capital, Albany, and

★

back again. The *Clermont* was to carry 40 passengers on its first voyage. They included Fulton, Livingston, other men who had invested in the boat and friends.

That morning Fulton was up early and on board the *Clermont* just after dawn. The boat's firebox was readied. By ten o'clock the boiler was fully heated and the steam engine chugging away. The boat's passengers began to arrive. Nearly all of them were frightened by the *Clermont's* massive machinery. Many thought the boat might be dangerous. Most of them were afraid of Fulton's boat failing, their investment being lost and all the people onshore laughing them out of the water. By 1:00 P.M. all the passengers were on board, however. The time had come for Fulton and his *Clermont* to show America what they could do.

The dock line was cast off. The boat's big brass bell clanged. Great clouds of smoke poured out of the boat's 30-foot-tall smokestack. The boat's engineer opened a valve, and the boat began to move away from the dock. The passengers watched all this action nervously. Then, under its own power, the boat began to move. And then, suddenly, the *Clermont's* engine died.

From shore came the laughter of some of the onlookers. Was this day to bring to Fulton the same bad luck John Fitch had experienced nearly 20 years earlier? Was Fulton to be laughed off the river and his boat considered a failure and a joke?

Robert Fulton immediately leaped onto one of the boat's seats and spoke to the people on board. He did not know what was wrong, he told them, but he promised to fix the problem in less than 30 minutes. And he did! After he had made a few minor adjustments to the engine, the *Clermont* was soon producing steam and heading upriver. The passengers sighed in

★

40

relief. Those people lined along the dock cheered. A United States flag, with its circle of 15 stars, waved proudly from the ship's mast in a northern breeze. Steaming along at 5 miles an hour, the *Clermont* headed for Albany.

The voyage was a pleasant one after all. Fulton and Livingston treated their passengers to a great feast of ham, roast chicken, gingerbread, pound cake and fruit from the Livingston orchards. The *Clermont* made only a few stops along the way to take on firewood. There was not enough deck space to carry all the wood the steamboat needed for the entire trip. That night the passengers sang together. At the day's end, the women went below to sleep in the steamboat's cabin. The men stayed on deck and tried to get some sleep. The next morning breakfast was served and the *Clermont* continued its trip upriver.

After a full 24 hours of traveling up the Hudson River, Fulton docked his steamboat at Robert Livingston's estate, Clermont-on-the-Hudson. The boat had covered 110 miles. The passengers spent the rest of the day enjoying Livingston's hospitality. They passed a comfortable night, away from the noises of the river and the *Clermont*'s chugging steam engine.

The next day, Wednesday, Fulton steamed his boat into Albany at 5:00 P.M. The running time for this first voyage of Fulton's steamboat was 32 hours. The boat had achieved a speed of 5 miles an hour, moving against the Hudson River's current. The return trip took only 30 travel hours, not including an hour's stop at Clermont-on-the-Hudson. Fulton returned to New York City in triumph.

Over the following weeks, Robert Fulton made improvements and changes on his steamboat. He added 12 sleeping berths and charged seven dollars per person to carry passengers up and down the Hudson. On September 4, the *Clermont* made its first public passenger trip. All the berths were paid for on this voyage. Eventually, the *Clermont* was enlarged to carry as many as 90 passengers at a time. With each one paying seven dollars, it is easy to see why Robert Fulton's steamboat soon became the first commercially profitable steamboat in American history.

Fulton and Livingston continued their partnership for several more years. They added other steamboats to their Hudson River fleet. The *Car of Neptune* was finished in 1809, and a third boat, called the *Paragon,* quickly followed. Before his death in 1815, Robert Fulton designed and built nine other passenger steamboats. One of these, the *Emperor of Russia,* was built for use in Europe. He also built two ferryboats, the *York* and the *Nassau,* which were used to carry horses and carriages across the East River. In addition, Fulton designed and built the first steam warship, called *Fulton the First.*

Within four years of the successful launching of the *Clermont,* another partner of Fulton and Livingston's, Nicholas Roosevelt, built a steamboat in Pittsburgh called the *New Orleans.* In 1811 Roosevelt steamed his boat down the Ohio River to the Mississippi and south to the city of New Orleans. By 1817 two steamboats had been launched on the Great Lakes. One was a Canadian boat, the *Frontenac,* and an American vessel, the *Ontario,* was the other. With the success of these and many other steamboats, the age of steam on America's vast river and lake system had arrived, all within ten years of Robert Fulton's success on the Hudson in a steamboat called the *Clermont.*

Passengers were able to relax and enjoy themselves while traveling on a steamboat.

★

The Rivers
Keep Flowing

From 1820 until the beginning of the Civil War, steamboats regularly paddled up and down the Ohio and Mississippi rivers. Other rivers, from the Missouri to the Tennessee, saw riverboats as well. River steamers carried much of the cargo to market for the entire Mississippi Valley. For many years, New Orleans continued to be the most important port on the great Mississippi. By 1840 steamboats made up four-fifths of the water traffic on the western rivers and the Great Lakes.

Flatboats and keelboats, as well as other smaller rivercraft, continued to be widely used. Some American rivers became crowded with an assortment of steamers, barges, flatboats and other vessels. But much of that traffic came to an end during the Civil War. Steamboat traffic was over, and boats on the Mississippi entered the river at their own risk.

At the same time, the railroads were expanding

★

their service to the West, making much riverboat traffic unnecessary. By 1860, 30,000 miles of rail track connected the East with the western states and territories. Gone were the golden days of river travel on the Ohio and the Mississippi.

America's great river system is not relied upon today for transportation as it was in the nineteenth century. However, the days of early river travel remain an important part of American history.

★

For Further Reading

Crisman, Ruth. *The Mississippi*. New York: Franklin Watts, 1984.

Landau, Elaine. *Robert Fulton*. New York: Franklin Watts, 1991.

Stein, Conrad R. *The Story of Mississippi Steamboats*. Chicago: Childrens Press, 1987.

Tunis, Edwin. *Colonial Living*. New York: HarperCollins Children's Books, 1976.

Tunis, Edwin. *Oars, Sails and Steam: A Picture Book of Ships*. New York: World Publishing Company, 1977.

Tunis, Edwin. *Wheels: A Pictorial History*. New York: HarperCollins Children's Books, 1977.

Glossary

birchbark canoe—Type of Indian canoe made from strips of birchbark sewn together and sealed for waterproofing.

black spruce gum—Sticky sap taken from the black spruce tree. It was used to seal (waterproof) birchbark canoes.

broadhorn—Also called sweep. It was a large paddle used to steer a flatboat.

canoe—A light boat with pointed ends, propelled by paddles.

cordelle—To pull a keelboat upriver by using ropes and pulleys.

dugout—Type of Indian canoe in which a log is hollowed out by carving or by fire.

gouger—A smaller flatboat paddle usually placed at the front of the boat. This sweep was another aid in steering the boat.

Northwest Ordinance—This act of Congress allowed for government in the territories of the Northwest, later the states of Ohio, Indiana, Illinois, Michigan and Wisconsin. The ordinance allowed for a survey of the territory as well.

Ohio Valley—The western land bordered by the Great Lakes to the north, the Appalachian Mountains to the east, the Mississippi River to the west and the Gulf coast to the south.

Proclamation of 1763—Law passed by the British Parliament which made it illegal for English colonists in America to travel across the Appalachian Mountains in the Ohio Valley. The act reserved that area for the Indians.

propulsion—The power to drive forward.

steamboats—Boats powered by a steam engine and paddle wheels.

stern—Rear part of a ship or boat.

sweeps—Also called broadhorns.

tributaries—Branches of a river.

Index

★